The Urbanization of
American Indians

BIBLIOGRAPHICAL SERIES
*The Newberry Library Center
for the History of the American Indian*

General Editor
Francis Jennings

Assistant Editor
William R. Swagerty

The Center Is Supported by Grants from

The National Endowment for the Humanities
The Ford Foundation
The W. Clement and Jessie V. Stone Foundation
The Woods Charitable Fund, Inc.
Mr. Gaylord Donnelley
The Andrew W. Mellon Foundation
The Robert R. McCormick Charitable Trust
The John D. and Catherine T. McArthur Foundation

The Urbanization of American Indians

A Critical Bibliography

RUSSELL THORNTON
GARY D. SANDEFUR
HAROLD G. GRASMICK

Published for the Newberry Library

Indiana University Press

BLOOMINGTON

Manufactured in the United States of America

Library of Congress Cataloging in Publication Data

Thornton, Russell, 1942–
    The urbanization of American Indians.

    (Bibliographical series / The Newberry Library Center for the History of the American Indian)
    Includes index.
    1. Indians of North America — Urban residence — Bibliography. 2. Indians of North America — Social conditions — Bibliography. I. Sandefur, Gary D., 1951– . II. Grasmick, Harold G., 1947– . III. Title. IV. Series: Bibliographical series (Newberry Library. Center for the History of the American Indian)
Z1209.T47 [E98.U72]   016.97'000497   81–48087
ISBN 0–253–36205–9 (pbk.)   AACR2
1 2 3 4 5 86 85 84 83 82

CONTENTS

ACKNOWLEDGMENTS

We wish to acknowledge able bibliographical contributions by Linda J. Kangas of the University of Minnesota and Linda McCabe of the University of Oklahoma. The Administration for Native American Research Analysis Project (ANARAP) of the University of Oklahoma, codirected by Phil Lujan, Brooks Hill, and William Carmack, also provided invaluable assistance. The work of Russell Thornton was done under the auspices of a Research Scientist Career Development Award from the National Institute of Mental Health. The work of Gary D. Sandefur and Harold G. Grasmick was done under the auspices of the University of Oklahoma's Applied Sociology for Urban Native American Agencies training program, of which they are codirectors, funded by the National Institute of Mental Health. The bibliography itself is an outgrowth of The 1980 Annual Conference on Problems and Issues concerning American Indians Today, the Newberry Library Center for the History of the American Indian, Chicago, Illinois (see [128]).

RECOMMENDED WORKS

For the Beginner

[15]   Ruth Blumenfeld, "Mohawks: Round Trip to the High Steel."

[57]   Melvin L. Fowler, "A Pre-Columbian Urban Center on the Mississippi."

[71]   Jeanne E. Guillemin, *Urban Renegades.*

[80]   Jorge E. Hardoy, *Pre-Columbian Cities.*

[168] Sol Tax, "The Impact of Urbanization on American Indians."

[188] Murray L. Wax, *Indian Americans: Unity and Diversity.*

For a Basic Library Collection

[35]   Sherburne F. Cook, *The Population of the California Indians, 1769–1970.*

[42]   Henry F. Dobyns, *Native American Historical Demography.*

[75]   Erna Gunther, *Indian Life on the Northwest Coast of North America.*

BIBLIOGRAPHICAL ESSAY

Introduction

The urbanization of American Indians is typically considered as a migration over the last few decades from rural areas and reservations to the present large cities of the United States and Canada. But this is only part of the phenomenon.

Urban areas of one form or another have been a facet of the life of various native peoples of the Western Hemisphere for thousands of years. Cities developed (independently, undoubtedly) in two regions of the world: the Mesopotamian region of the Eastern Hemisphere, and the Mesoamerican region of the Western Hemisphere, as Gideon Sjoberg has discussed in *The Preindustrial City* [151]. Using a somewhat restrictive definition, Kingsley Davis, in "The Origin and Growth of Urbanization in the World" [39], places the date of the first "cities" of the Eastern Hemisphere at some seven thousand to eight thousand years ago, and, using an even more restricted definition, places the date of the first "true cities" of that hemisphere at about five thousand years ago. Similarly, Jorge E. Hardoy, in *Pre-Columbian Cities* [80], develops a set of ten specific, restrictive criteria for cities and places the first in the Western Hemisphere at perhaps three thousand years ago.

Certainly no early city or urban area of either hemisphere compared in size with the largest cities of today. Considering, for example, the probable size of the early cities of the Eastern Hemisphere, Ur had a population of only about 5,000, Erech perhaps 25,000, Tell el 'Amarna some 40,000, and Thebes approximately 225,000, as Davis [39] indicates. Considering the probable size of the largest early cities of the Western Hemisphere, prehistoric Teotihuacán had a population of perhaps 85,000. Early sixteenth-century Tenochtitlán housed some 150,000 to 300,000 people and perhaps more and was one of the very largest cities in the world about A.D. 1500. The Inca capital Cuzco contained about 200,000 people, with possibly another 200,000 in close proximity, as Hardoy [80] discusses.

The native peoples of the area now called the United States and Canada also developed population concentrations, cities, and urban areas, though they were surely neither as early nor as large as those to the south. These peoples developed, for example, Moundville (Alabama), Pueblo Bonita (New Mexico), and Cahokia (Illinois, just across the Mississippi River from present-day Saint Louis). Probably the largest of these was Cahokia; it attained a population of about 40,000 some eight hundred years ago, as indicated by Melvin L. Fowler in "A Pre-Columbian Urban Center on the Mississippi" [57].

Of course these population concentrations of the original people of this land have now ceased to exist as such. The decline of many American Indian population centers may be traced to European contact and the native population reduction it produced, often from smallpox and other European diseases, as mentioned regarding Cherokee towns by James Mooney in *Histori-*

cal Sketch of the Cherokee [123] and as described graphically regarding a Mandan village by George Catlin in *Letters and Notes on the Manners, Customs, and Conditions of North American Indians* [20]. (See Henry F. Dobyns's *Native American Historical Demography: A Critical Bibliography* [42] in this series for a detailed discussion of this population history.)

Aside from having developed their own urban areas, American Indians became involved very early in the post-Columbian cities built by Europeans and others on this land. American Indians were, for example, involved with several California cities, particularly those growing from early missions, as discussed broadly by Sherburne F. Cook in his "Migration and Urbanization of the Indians in California" [28], his *The Conflict between the California Indians and White Civilization* [33], and his *The Population of the California Indians, 1769–1970* [35], and as discussed specifically regarding the missions by James R. Young, Dennis Moristo, and G. David Tenebaum in *An Inventory of the Mission Indian Agency Records* [198] and by James P. Ronda and James Axtell in *Indian Missions: A Critical Bibliography* [145]. American Indians were also, for example, involved in many of the early cities and towns in Oklahoma, as discussed in United States Bureau of the Census, *The Five Civilized Tribes in Indian Territory* [175] and *Population of Oklahoma and Indian Territory: 1907* [176], and in Arizona as discussed by Henry F. Dobyns regarding Tucson in his *Spanish Colonial Tucson* [43].

Also, recent American Indian urbanization did not

occur only within the largest of the cities of the United States and Canada. The definition of urban, for example, used by the United States Bureau of the Census for the 1970 and 1980 censuses [177] is rather broad, with an urban area often including several small cities and towns:

> The urban population comprises all persons living in urban areas. More specifically, the urban population consists of all persons living in (a) places of 2,500 inhabitants or more incorporated as cities, villages, boroughs (except Alaska), and towns (except in the New England States, New York, and Wisconsin), but excluding those persons living in the rural portions of extended cities; (b) unincorporated places of 2,500 inhabitants or more; and (c) other territory, incorporated or unincorporated, included in urbanized areas. The population not classified as urban constitutes the rural population.
>
> An urbanized area, generally, consists of at least one city of 50,000 inhabitants or more in 1970 and the surrounding closely settled area that meets certain criteria of population density or land use. An urbanized area may be subdivided into the central city or cities, and the remainder of the area as "urban fringes." The central city portion, generally, consists of the population of the city or cities named in the title of the urbanized area.

Calvin L. Beale, in "Migration Patterns of Minorities in the United States" [10], indicates that in 1970 only 60 percent of urbanized Indians lived in central cities, whereas 84 percent of urbanized Blacks did. Thus contemporary American Indian urbanization encompasses suburban areas and small cities and towns and villages as well as large cities.

The urbanization of American Indians also includes more than the simple movement of American Indians to urban areas, though this has surely been important. It includes differential, nonmigratory population growth of urban areas versus other areas. There are two ways populations grow and decline: through differences in births and deaths, and through migration. The urbanization of American Indians is a phenomenon of differential fertility and mortality of American Indians in urban and nonurban areas *and* of differential migration between these areas. (In terms of official statistics, differences in definition and enumeration procedures may also occasionally be involved.)

Finally, American Indian urbanization is not only a physical occurrence. It is also a social and cultural process whereby the values and norms of urbanism are transmitted to Indian peoples in nonurban areas through television, radio, printed matter, and other means of mass communication. In certain cultural respects, American Indians have undoubtedly thus become urbanized without direct contact with urban areas. (Conversely, however, as will be discussed later in this bibliography, the physical location of American Indians in urban areas does not necessarily mean that they accept the "ways of life" they encounter there.)

We have attempted to discuss these various facets of American Indian urbanization, though we do not

claim expertise in all of them. We generally limit our-
selves to American Indians of the United States and
Canada and emphasize their involvement in large
twentieth-century cities, as this is the focus of most of
the existing literature. We give representative examples
of available literature; we have not attempted to be
exhaustive in detailing the literature of any particular
area. Furthermore, we use an extremely broad
definition of what constitutes "urban," and we consider
various types of population concentrations, including
villages and towns as well as cities themselves.

American Indian Cities, Towns, and Villages

Pre-Columbian Cities of Middle and South America

A variety of general works on pre-Columbian cities
south of the Rio Grande are to be found. These in-
clude Jorge E. Hardoy's *Urban Planning in Pre-
Columbian America* [81] and his work mentioned earlier,
Pre-Columbian Cities [80]. The latter is a good introduc-
tion to the various urban centers of that time and
place, including Teotihuacán, and Tula, Xochicalo,
Monte Alban, and Mitla after the fall of Teotihuacán,
Tenochtitlán, the Mayan "cities" of Cobá, Copán,
Chichén Itzá, and Tikal, and the South American
Tiahuanaco, Marca Huamachuco, Chan Chan, and, of
course, Cuzco, Tambo Colorado, and Machu Picchu.

More recent general accounts of the history of
these peoples and their cities may be found in T. Pat-

rick Culbert's "Mesoamerica" [38] and his *The Lost Civilization: The Story of the Classic Maya* [37] and in Michael E. Moseley's "The Evolution of Andean Civilization" [125].

Discussions of specific pre-Columbian cities of this area are also widely available, perhaps more so for Teotihuacán than for any other city. As René Millon points out in "Teotihuacán" [122], the city covered an area larger than imperial Rome, had more than four thousand buildings, mostly apartment houses, and had a probable population of at least 100,000 (and perhaps close to 200,000). Its development and decline are discussed by John Pfeiffer in his "The Life and Death of a Great City" [136]. Chan Chan, the great city of the Andes, is discussed by Michael E. Moseley in his "Chan Chan: Andean Alternative to the Pre-Industrial City" [124].

A specific discussion of the importance of the development of agriculture, particularly *zea mays* (corn), to the growth of these early cities may be found in "The Origins of New World Civilization" [117], by Richard S. MacNeish.

Pre- and Post-Columbian Settlements North of the Rio Grande

Though they were undoubtedly nowhere as large as those to the south, pre-Columbian urban areas, cities, and other population concentrations also existed north of the Rio Grande.

Surely the largest of these was just to the east of present-day Saint Louis. It is named Cahokia (after the Indians living in the area of the city at the time of French colonization early in the eighteenth century) and served as a trade and transportation center. During the period of its highest development—some eight hundred years ago—its population was probably close to 40,000. Cahokia declined after that, however, reaching a final phase during the two-hundred-year period following Columbus's initital contact with this hemisphere. This decline may have been related to the exhaustion of local resources such as timber, game animals, and fertile land for growing maize, and to the growth of other centers in the area; but just why and how it occurred is now unknown.

A good account of Cahokia is the one mentioned previously by Melvin L. Fowler [57]. A more popular account is John Pfeiffer's "America's First City" [135]. Another description of Cahokia, as well as of other cities and towns of the Mississippi area, may be found in James B. Griffin's "The Midlands and Northeastern United States" [69], and in J. Joseph Bauxar's "History of the Illinois Area" [9].

Griffin also briefly discusses settlements to the north and east of this area, including the Iroquoian Hochelaga, with a population of about 2,000 near the start of the Columbian period, and the Huron Cahiague, with a population of some 5,000 for the same general period. Hochelaga and other Iroquoian settlements are discussed by Bruce G. Trigger and

James F. Pendergast in "Saint Lawrence Iroquoians" [173], and other Huron settlements are described by Conrad E. Heidenreich in "Huron" [84], including Teanaustaye, with a population of some 2,800, and Ossossane, with a population of about 1,400.

Finally, other discussions of American Indian settlements of this region may be found in *Notes on the Iroquois; or, Contributions to the Statistics, Aboriginal History, Antiquities and General Ethnology of Western New York* by Henry R. Schoolcraft [148]; "Ancient Tribes Revisited: A Summary of Indian Distribution and Movement in the Northeastern United States from 1534 to 1779" by Bernard G. Hoffman [91]; and *The Indian Population of New England in the Seventeenth Century* by Sherburne F. Cook [34].

There were also fairly large American Indian population concentrations to the north, though not actual cities, as discussed by W. Raymond Wood, for example, in "Northern Plains Village Cultures: Internal Stability and External Relationships" [196]. Some concentrations existing more recently were reported by George Catlin [20]. He mentions Sioux encampments with six hundred tents, encampments of several thousand Assiniboines, an Iowa village of 1,400, and a Pawnee village of five hundred to six hundred houses. Catlin also gives a detailed account of his visit to a great Comanche village of from six hundred to eight hundred lodges containing thousands of people.

In the southeastern part of what is now the United States, there were also sizable early American Indian settlements. As discussed by Jon D. Muller in "The Southeast" [126], there were, for example, Moundville (Alabama) and Etowah (Georgia).

The importance of such settlements then and in the subsequent life of the Indians of the Southeast may be illustrated by the Cherokees. Cherokees often refer to themselves as people of Ketoowah, after an ancient Cherokee town, and Cherokee clans may be traced to seven early "mother" towns. Very early Cherokee towns are discussed by Gary C. Goodwin in *Cherokee in Transition: A Study of Changing Culture and Environment prior to 1775* [61], and more recent communities are discussed by Douglas C. Wilms in his "Cherokee Settlement Patterns in Nineteenth Century Georgia" [193]. (See also *The Cherokees: A Critical Bibliography,* by Raymond D. Fogelson [54], in this series.)

Perhaps best known among the early American Indian settlements are those of the Southwest, the cliff dwellings and pueblos. Probably the most famous of these and one of the largest was Pueblo Bonito in the Chaco Canyon of northeastern New Mexico. It attained a population approaching 3,000 people some one thousand years ago. Other large pueblos of the same period and general area were Chetco Ketl and Pueblo del Arroyo, within the canyon, and Pueblo Pintado and the Salmon Ruin, outside the canyon. These and other settlements are discussed in William D. Lipe, "The Southwest" [112], one of several chapters cited in this bibliography from Jesse D. Jennings, ed., *Ancient Native Americans* [97].

Somewhat later—from about seven hundred to

about four hundred years ago—there were fewer but probably generally larger settlements, including Teewi and Sapawe. A recent source of information on these settlements as well as on the entire history and contemporary situation of the people of this area is found in Alfonso Ortiz, ed., *Southwest,* volume 9 of the *Handbook of North American Indians* [130].

Moving further to the west, there were also fairly large pre-European population concentrations including those of the Pomos, easily surpassing village sizes of 1,000 to 1,500, and the somewhat smaller ones of the Chumashes and others. These are discussed in Robert F. Heizer, ed., *California,* volume 8 of the *Handbook of North American Indians* [85]. Early reports of some of these and other settlements and their sizes, as well as subsequent analysis by the author, may be found in Sherburne F. Cook's "The Aboriginal Population of the San Joaquin Valley, California" [29], "The Aboriginal Population of the North Coast of California" [30], "The Aboriginal Population of Alameda and Contra Costa Counties, California" [31], and "Colonial Expeditions to the Interior of California, Central Valley, 1800–1820" [32]. Martin A. Baumhoff's "California Athabascan Groups" [8] also discusses village sizes as well as other issues. Finally, the book by Sherburne Cook on the history of the California Indian population [35] is a detailed examination of the population history of these peoples, including their more recent urbanization in the large contemporary urban areas of California.

Discussions of early settlements in the Pacific

Northwest may be found in Marian W. Smith's *Indians of the Urban Northwest* [152]; in the *Original Journals of the Lewis and Clark Expeditions 1804–1806* edited by Reuben Gold Thwaites [172]; and, particularly, in Erna Gunther's *Indian Life on the Northwest Coast of North America* [75].

Twentieth Century Urbanization

Trend toward Urbanization

Although scholars still debate the size of the pre-European American Indian population (and perhaps will always do so), it was undoubtedly at least several million for the area north of the Rio Grande. With the arrival of the Europeans on this continent, there commenced a drastic reduction of the American Indian population. Because of new diseases (particularly smallpox) introduced by the Europeans, genocide, population relocation, warfare, and destruction of ways of life, the American Indian population declined to only a few hundred thousand by the beginning of the twentieth century. (This is discussed by Russell Thornton and Joan Marsh-Thornton in "Estimating Prehistoric American Indian Population Size for the United States Area: Implications of the Nineteenth Century Population Decline and Nadir" [171].) Coinciding with this population decline was a decline in the cities, towns, and villages of American Indians.

Since the beginning of this century, the American

Indian population has increased steadily. As this increase has occurred, so has a redistribution from rural to urban areas. These twentieth-century urban areas are typically not those of Indian peoples themselves but those of another social and cultural system (though the pueblos continue to exist as villages and there are small "Indian towns" in reservation areas and in parts of Oklahoma) as discussed for the Cherokees by Albert L. Wahrhaftig in "The Tribal Cherokee Population of Eastern Oklahoma" [186].

In Table 1 (from Alan L. Sorkin's *The Urban American Indian* [157]), data are presented showing both this population growth and the increased urbanization for the United States. The 1980 census enumeration will likely reaffirm the estimate for 1977, showing, in 1980, more than one million American Indians in the United States, over half living in urban areas.

Census data pertaining to this urbanization have been analyzed in United States Department of Health, Education, and Welfare, *A Study of Selected Socio-Economic Characteristics of Ethnic Minorities Based on the 1970 Census* [179], and in Calvin Beale's paper referred to earlier [10]. Beale points out that during the decade 1960–70, the rural American Indian population grew only 16 percent, whereas the urban Indian population grew by 144 percent.

In the remainder of this bibliography we discuss scholarly literature pertaining to this recent urbanization, its causes, and its effects on American Indians and their ways of life.

Table 1

Total, Urban, and Rural American Indian
Population in the United States (to
nearest thousand), 1890–1977

Year	Total	Urban	Rural	Percentage Urban
1890	248,000	—	—	—
1900	237,000	1,000	236,000	0.4
1910	266,000	12,000	254,000	4.5
1920	244,000	15,000	229,000	6.1
1930	332,000	33,000	299,000	9.9
1940	334,000	24,000	310,000	7.2
1950	343,000	56,000	287,000	13.4
1960	524,000	146,000	378,000	27.9
1970	764,000	340,000	424,000	44.5
1977[a]	1,000,000	500,000	500,000	50.0

Note: Some of the data reported here are based on census samples, not total enumerations. The total United States American Indian population reported in the census of 1970 was 792,730; the figure 764,000 reported here is from the 20 percent sample.

[a]Estimated.

American Indians in Cities: General Considerations

A variety of rather general works on the urbanization of American Indians may be found in the literature. These include William H. Hodge's *The Albuquer-*

que Navajos [89]; Elaine M. Neils's *Reservation to City* [127]; Jeanne E. Guillemin's *Urban Renegades* [71]; parts of Murray L. Wax's *Indian Americans: Unity and Diversity* [188]; and Sorkin's book referred to earlier [157]. An excellent general introduction (though now somewhat dated) is *The American Indian in Urban Society,* edited by Jack O. Waddell and O. Michael Watson [183].

During the late 1960s and early 1970s, the Center for Urban and Regional Affairs at the University of Minnesota sponsored various studies of American Indians in such cities as Duluth, Minneapolis, Dallas, Chicago, and Omaha. Most of these are listed in Arthur M. Harkins's *A Bibliography of Urban Indians in the United States* [82].

Other relevant works are *Final Report to the American Indian Policy Review Commission of Task Force Eight on Urban and Rural Non-Reservation Indians* [167] and sections of *The Sociology of American Indians: A Critical Bibliography* [170] by Russell Thornton and Mary K. Grasmick.

Determinants of Rural-to-Urban Migration

A variety of factors seem to influence rural-to-urban migration, as we shall see. However, equally important to the topic is movement back to rural areas after migration to urban ones.

In "The Migration and Adaptation of American Indians to Los Angeles" [137], John A. Price suggests that one of the keys to the size of rural-to-urban migration after 1955 is the Bureau of Indian Affairs' "relocation program." This program began in 1950 when the BIA hired placement officers in four areas. (See James E. Officer's "The American Indian and Federal Policy" [129].) Under the program, the BIA assists American Indian people in moving from their reservations to selected urban areas. After the move, the BIA provides employment counseling and other forms of assistance, including vocational training and education. One of the urban areas selected for the relocation program was Los Angeles, which now has the largest urban American Indian population in the United States.

This program has not been responsible for all American Indian migration to urban areas, and perhaps only about 100,000 people were directly moved under the program in its first twenty years, as Arthur Margon suggests in "Indians and Immigrants: A Comparison of Groups New to the City" [119]. Also, not all those relocated stayed in urban areas. (The return rate is estimated by Margon at somewhere between 30 percent and 70 percent.) However, the BIA effort has certainly been an important factor in urbanization during the past few decades and has received considerable attention.

An early report of the relocation program is cited in Francis Paul Prucha's edited work, *Documents of United States Indian Policy* [139] (it is from the 1954 *Annual Report of the Commissioner of Indian Affairs* [178]):

During the 1954 fiscal year, 2,163 Indians were directly assisted to relocate under the Bureau's relocation program. This included 1,649 persons in over 400 family groups, and 514 unattached men and women. In addition, over 300 Indians left reservations without assistance to join relatives and friends who had been assisted to relocate. At their destination, Bureau Relocation Offices assisted this group also to adjust to the new community. The total number of relocations represented a substantial increase over relocations during the previous fiscal year.

Of the 2,163 Indians assisted to relocate, financial assistance, to cover all or part of the costs of transportation to the place of relocation and short-term temporary subsistence, was provided to 1,637 Indians, in addition to relocation services. This number included 1,329 persons in over 300 family groups, and 308 unattached men and women. An additional 526 Indians, including 320 in approximately 100 family groups and 206 unattached men and women, were assisted to relocate without financial assistance, but were provided relocation services only. These services included counseling and guidance prior to relocation, and assistance in establishing residence and securing permanent employment in the community. . . .

Approximately 54 percent of the Indians assisted to relocate came from 3 northern areas (Aberdeen, Billings, and Minneapolis), and 46 percent came from 4 southern areas (Anadarko, Gallup, Muskogee, and Phoenix). They went to 20 different States. The Los Angeles and Chicago metropolitan areas continued to be the chief centers of relocation.

Although federally sponsored relocation was surely not the major reason for recent increases in American Indian urbanization, increases in urbanization of American Indians, as indicated Table 1, were fairly modest until 1950. Along with this sponsored relocation, however, other factors leading to increased urbanization were the transmission of urban values and culture through education and the mass media and the trend toward replacing native languages with English. Urbanization has increased considerably since 1950, particularly between 1950 and 1970. Increases from 1970 to 1977 were less dramatic, it seems; however, the time span is three years shorter, and figures for 1977 are only estimated. It will be interesting to see what the 1980 census enumeration shows in this regard.

In "Alternative Models for the Study of Urban Migration" [61], Theodore D. Graves discusses three models that might be used to examine who participates in relocation (as well as other aspects of American Indian rural-to-urban migration). One of these is termed the "decision model," since it emphasizes personality variables as the major determinants of migration. A second, referred to as the "assimilation model," emphasizes social group membership, individual identity, and interaction patterns. The third model, the "economic adjustment model," focuses on individual training and skills as the most important determinants of moving to, and remaining in, urban areas.

In "'Push' and 'Pull' Factors: Reasons for Migration as a Factor in American Indian Urban Adjustment" [101], James N. Kerri points out that it is often useful to distinguish between factors in the area of origin that cause individuals to leave a rural area or reservation and factors in the area of destination that draw individuals to urban areas. Sam Stanley and Robert K. Thomas, in "Current Demographic and Social Trends among North American Indians" [158], differentiate three types of Indian migrants: (1) those who remain oriented to their home reservations, moving back and forth between reservation and city; (2) those who are skilled laborers, living generally on the fringes of urban areas; and (3) the "Indian middle class," living in predominantly White neighborhoods, but often remaining active in Indian cultural and political activities.

Research using these and other analytical models suggests that the major factor involved in American Indian migration to urban areas may be economic opportunity. There appear to be two primary reasons for this: there is a lack of job opportunities on most reservations and in many rural areas where Indians live; and American Indians tend to perceive urban areas as having good employment opportunities (whether or not it is the case).

Thus, Price [137] finds that the major incentive for migration is economic: Indians moved to urban areas because they were interested in jobs, or better jobs, higher wages, and improved living conditions. These findings are basically supported by Theodore D. Graves in "The Personal Adjustment of Navajo Indian

Migrants to Denver, Colorado" [64] and by Arthur Margon's paper cited earlier [119]. Somewhat along these lines, an interesting article discussing the development of an American Indian urban occupation is William Hodge's "Navaho Urban Silversmiths" [88].

There are various other reasons why American Indians move to urban areas, however. Joseph D. Bloom, in "Migration and Psychopathology of Eskimo Women" [14], suggests that many Eskimo women move to urban areas because they are dissatisfied with their subordinate role in Eskimo society. In "When the Indian Comes to the City" [189], Gene Weltfish suggest that perceived educational/training opportunities are important.

Similarly, there are often established American Indian communities in urban areas that operate both to attract migrants and to facilitate their movement. This has been important in the continued migration of Navajos to Los Angeles, as Calvin Beale suggests [10]. Similarly, John Gregory Peck, in "Urban Station–Migration of the Lumbee Indians" [134], illustrates how an enclave of Lumbees in Baltimore has made that city an attractive place for potential Lumbee migrants. Also relevant in this regard is John A. Price's "U.S. and Canadian Indian Urban Ethnic Institutions" [138].

Though there appears substantial agreement on why American Indians migrate to urban areas, there appears somewhat less agreement on why some remain and others leave.

Theodore D. Graves and Minor van Arsdale, for

example, argue, in "Values, Expectations and Relocation: The Navajo Migrant to Denver" [68], that the only reasons Indians stay in cities are the economic advantages there. Thus they find in their study that "economic-material goals" of Navajos in Denver are more salient for those remaining in Denver than for those leaving the city. They find, however, no differences between those staying in Denver and those leaving in the importance of "social love-affection goals" or in the importance of traditional Navajo culture and activities. Alan L. Sorkin, in "Some Aspects of American Indian Migration" [155], finds that more highly educated Indians are more likely to migrate to urban areas, more likely to participate in adult vocational training and direct training programs, and more likely to remain in the urban environment than are less educated Indians. According to Sorkin, this is because the more educated are more economically successful than the less educated. Similarly, in "Correlates of Adjustment among American Indians in an Urban Environment" [120], Harry W. Martin finds that younger, more educated, "mixed-blood" Indians—in sum, those who earned more money—were more likely to remain in urban areas than others. Supportive results are discussed by Robert Weppner in "Urban Economic Opportunities: The Example of Denver" [190].

Conversely, Bruce A. Chadwick and Lynn C. White find, in "Correlates of Length of Urban Residence among the Spokane Indians" [23], that degree of Indian ancestry and degree of Indian self-identification are most important in explaining why some Indians leave Spokane and return to their reservations. (See also the study "The Measurement of Assimilation: The Spokane Indians," by Prodipto Roy [147].) In "The Role of Intermarriage in the Acculturation of Selected Urban American Indian Women" [185], Jean K. Wagner argues that intermarriage with Whites results in more rapid assimilation and acculturation, which in turn make intermarried American Indian women more likely to remain in urban areas.

Despite these somewhat divergent findings, the evidence seems to suggest that economic factors are probably most important in determining whether American Indians remain in urban situations after they have migrated to them. Those satisfied with their jobs, earnings, and living conditions are quite simply less likely than those who are dissatisfied to leave cities and suburbs and return to rural areas or reservations. American Indians may not like cities or urban areas in general, but they do appear to tolerate life there if they have satisfactory employment and income.

For those who return, however, the move may not be permanent, just as the original move to an urban area was not permanent. Many American Indians exhibit a pattern of "circular" migration whereby they spend periods of time in urban areas, then return to nonurban areas, then move again to urban areas and so forth. Wesley R. Hurt, Jr. [94] describes this pattern among Sioux from Yankton and Santee reservations in the 1950s as they moved temporarily into Yankton,

South Dakota, for seasonal jobs. This pattern of capitalizing on economic opportunities is further discussed in Ruth Blumenfeld's "Mohawks: Round Trip to the High Steel" [15]; Sol Tax's "The Impact of Urbanization on American Indians" [168]; and Jack O. Waddell's *Papago Indians at Work* [181].

Other related research pertaining to reasons for migrating (and staying) may be found in Trevor Denton's "Migration from a Canadian Indian Reserve" [40]; David E. W. Holden's "Modernization among Town and Bush Cree in Quebec" [92]; and Peter Z. Snyder's "Social Interaction Patterns and Relative Urban Success: The Denver Navajo" [154]. Also see [18] and [102].

Demographic Trends

There has been little actual research on American Indian demographic trends, in part owing to scarcity of published data on American Indian population characteristics and vital events. It is thus often impossible to study American Indian demography with the same data sources (e.g., census reports) used to study other groups. Despite this problem, some research has been conducted on American Indian population growth, fertility and mortality trends, accident rates, and rates of disease.

Basic to this demographic research, in urban areas or elsewhere, is the definition and identification of the "American Indian" population. James L. Simmons discusses this in "One Little, Two Little, Three Little Indi-

ans: Counting American Indians in Urban Society"
[150]. He points out that there are at least six different
ways of identifying American Indians in urban areas
for purposes of enumeration. These are: (1) legal
definitions, for example, definitions used by the BIA,
Office of Indian Education, for title IV programs; (2)
self-identification (as currently used by the United
States Bureau of the Census); (3) recognition as Indian
by the local American Indian community or tribal unit;
(4) perceptions by non-Indians; (5) "blood" quantum;
and (6) use of a cultural definition or requirement.
Some of these issues are also considered by Jeffrey S.
Passell in his "Provisional Evaluation of the 1970 Census Count of American Indians" [133]; and by Albert
L. Wahrhaftig and Robert K. Thomas in their "Renais-
sance and Repression: The Oklahoma Cherokee"
[187]. (For a discussion of American Indian enumeration issues and procedures and the 1980 census, see
Lawrence S. Rosen and Kurt Gorwitz's "New Attention
to American Indians" [146].)

Regardless of how American Indians are identified (or counted), research suggests that the primary
reason for the recent population growth of both rural
and urban American Indian populations is a high
birthrate and declining rate of mortality (which is be-
coming progressively lower each year). Articles making
this simple but important point are Margot Liberty,
David V. Hughey, and Richard Scaglion's "Rural and
Urban Omaha Indian Fertility" [111]; A. Romaniuk's
"Modernization and Fertility: The Case of the James

Bay Indians" [143]; and Julie M. Uhlman's "The Impact of Modernization on Papago Indian Fertility" [174]. Research often shows, as Uhlmann points out, that the birthrate is considerably lower for urban American Indian women than for rural ones. However, the study by Liberty, Hughey, and Scaglion [111] disputes this finding, and of course part of this is due to the differential migration of unmarried, childless females to urban areas. It seems likely, though, that increased urbanization will lead to lower fertility rates for American Indians and (coupled with the eventual stability of mortality rates) a lower rate of American Indian population growth for the future.

Only scant research exists on the effect of urbanization on mortality. However, available data seem to indicate that urbanization results in better health care, resulting in the lower incidence of most diseases and a decreased mortality rate. See, for example, Carruth J. Wagner and Erwin S. Rabeau's "Indian Poverty and Indian Health" [184], which finds that accident rates of the Papago were lower in traditional communities than in urban areas. Similarly, Robert A. Hackenberg and Mary M. Gallagher find, in their "The Costs of Cultural Change: Accidental Injury and Modernization among the Papago Indians" [77], higher accident rates in "modern" Papago villages than in "traditional" ones. (Their methods were questionable, however, as they relied on informant rankings that seemed to refer more to contact with Whites than to modernization.)

Various other studies examine the demographic

effect of urbanization on American Indians. Included are Gerald Littman's "Alcoholism, Illness and Social Pathology among American Indians in Transition" [113]; A. Romaniuk and V. Piché's "Natality Estimates for the Canadian Indians by Stable Population Models, 1900–1969" [144]; Jane Riblett Wilke's "The United States Population by Race and Urban-Rural Residence 1790–1970: Reference Tables" [192]; John H. Burma's "Interethnic Marriage in Los Angeles, 1948–59" [19]; Constantine Panunzio's "Intermarriage in Los Angeles, 1924–33" [131]; J. Nixon Hadley's "The Demography of the American Indians" [79]; C. Roderick Wilson's "Papago Indian Population Movement: An Index of Cultural Change" [194]; and Harvey Flad's "The City and the Longhouse: A Social Geography of American Indians in Syracuse, New York" [53] and "The Urban American Indians of Syracuse, New York: Human Exploration of Urban Ethnic Space" [52].

Urbanization and Economic Status

There is little doubt that, in objective economic terms, abject poverty is characteristic of American Indian life both on reservations and in rural areas. Approximately 50 percent of the American Indians on reservations have incomes below the poverty line, as described by Alan L. Sorkin in his article, "The Economic Basis of Indian Life" [156]. The primary reasons are high levels of unemployment and underemployment. In effect, the American economy has bypassed

American Indian reservations, leaving Indians few opportunities to become productive members of the national labor force. As Joseph G. Jorgensen discusses in "A Century of Political Economic Effects on American Indian Society, 1880– 1980" [99], this is a result of the historical development of the American economy. In effect, American Indian resources were exploited (and often appropriated) without Indian people receiving any benefits from this development.

Ostensibly, the federal government recognized several years ago that measures were needed to improve the socioeconomic status of American Indians. Research tends to show, however, that urbanization does not necessarily improve economic conditions. For example, in a factual, noninterpretive description, *Indians in Minnesota* [108], the League of Women Voters of Minnesota noted that a 1972 study of all American Indian households known to the Indian Health Board in Minneapolis found that Aid to Dependent Children was the primary source of income for 55 percent, and employment was the main source for only 13 percent.

The success of federal efforts ultimately depends on the ability of programs and program administrators to deal adequately with the cultural and political context of American Indian life. As Robert L. Bee indicates in his study "Tribal Leadership in the War on Poverty: A Case Study" [11], program administrators are often very surprised by events that could easily have been anticipated if Indian politics and culture had been considered initially.

These factors need to be considered in urban situations as well. For example, Robert Weppner concludes in "Socioeconomic Barriers to Assimilation of Navajo Migrants" [191] that the lack of a notion of "scarcity" and the emphasis on "noncompetitiveness" and "nonaggressiveness" in Navajo society limit the success of Navajo migrants in an urban labor market. This in turn limits the success of BIA relocation efforts. A failure of BIA relocation programs to substantially reduce the poverty level of American Indians may very well be due in large part to a failure to consider unique American Indian political and cultural contexts.

However, there is research suggesting that relocation and urbanization can be very beneficial for certain types of American Indians while being less so (perhaps even harmful) for other types.

Lawrence Clinton, Bruce A. Chadwick, and Howard M. Bahr, in "Urban Relocation Reconsidered: Antecedents of Employment among Indian Males" [25], show that urban relocation results in improvement in employment opportunities, income, quality of housing, and perceived quality of life for many Indian people. Similarly, James H. Gundlach and Alden E. Roberts, in "Native American Indian Migration and Relocation: Success or Failure" [74], argue that, on the average, relocatees fare better than nonmigrants and other migrants. They argue further that the relocation program is useful in helping American Indians improve their lives, at least economically.

The crucial question, then, is, For which types of American Indians is relocation (or even nonassisted rural-to-urban migration) economically beneficial?

In "Migrants to the City: A Study of the Subeconomic Status of Native Americans in Detroit and Michigan" [13], Beatrice Anne Bigony reports that American Indian migrants to Detroit who have vocational skills are often quite successful in securing and retaining employment. In fact, not only do they tend to work steadily, but they also are more likely than those without such skills to live in nuclear family households, encourage their children to continue schooling, and have optimistic attitudes toward both work and life in general. Additionally, they tend to remain in Detroit and not return to reservations or rural places of origin.

Various other research findings support this idea that American Indians with skills and training are likely to benefit economically from living in urban areas. For example, Theodore D. Graves and Charles A. Lave report such findings in their "Determinants of Urban Migrant Indian Wages" [67]. They find that the major determinants of the starting wages of Navajo migrants to cities are education, highest wage before migration, vocational training, marital status, and whether their fathers were "wage laborers." Charles A. Lave, James V. Mueller, and Theodore D. Graves conclude that there is, however, a substantial threshold effect for education occurring at the ten-year mark. They find in their study "The Economic Payoff of Different Kinds of Education: A Study of Urban Migrants in Two Societies" [107] that formal education is not beneficial until one has attained at least ten years of schooling and, also, that economic payoff is higher for the same amount of "on-the-job" training and same amount of vocational training. Among factors hypothesized to be associated with economic success in urban areas but not found to be so by Lave, Mueller, and Graves was the possession of a "work ethic" and similar middle-class values. (This is discussed also by Theodore D. Graves in "Urban Indian Personality and the 'Culture of Poverty'" [66].) In a study mentioned earlier, however, Weppner [191] concludes that American Indians are able to adopt these middle-class traits quite readily, so they may be a consequence of economic stability and success rather than a cause of it.

In sum, educated, skilled, and married American Indian males are most likely to benefit economically from movement to urban areas.

Lawrence Clinton, Bruce A. Chadwick, and Howard M. Bahr's paper "Vocational Training for Indian Migrants: Correlates of 'Success' in a Federal Program" [24] contains data showing that males and individuals with employment experience are also more likely to successfully complete vocational training programs. Other research reaching essentially the same conclusions includes Joan Ablon's "American Indian Relocation: Problems of Dependency and Management in the City" [2]; Robert A. Hackenberg and C. Roderick Wilson's "Reluctant Emigrants: The Role of Migration in Papago Indian Adaptation" [78]; Lyle W. Shannon's

"The Economic Absorption and Cultural Integration of Immigrant Workers: Characteristics of the Individual versus the Nature of the System" [149]; and Fred Voget's "Introduction: American Indians and Their Economic Development" [180].

Because of problems with federally sponsored relocation, as well as pressure from tribal and reservation leaders, the federal government has encouraged both urban migration *and* reservation economic development. Problems with this "dual policy" are discussed by Robert L. Bee and R. Gingerich in "Colonialism, Classes, and Ethnic Identity: Native Americans and the National Political Economy" [12]. And, as Robert A. Hackenberg concludes in "Colorado River Basin Development and Its Potential Impact on Tribal Life" [76], those American Indians who are permanent urban residents will benefit little, if at all, from the development of reservation resources. It is also unlikely that this development will significantly influence the numbers of rural-to-urban migrants (see Sorkin [155]).

Though the BIA's relocation program is regarded by some as less than even a moderate success, or even as a failure, migration to urban areas enables many American Indians to escape poverty, unemployment, and underemployment. Only some 20 percent of urban Indians live below the poverty line compared with about 50 percent of those on reservations living below that level (see Sorkin [155]).

The Kinship System in the Urban Context

Considering the importance of kinship in traditional American Indian life and the abundance of anthropological research on it, surprisingly little research has been done on the Indian family in an urban setting. If the extended family is a crucial social and cultural component of Indian life, then surely it would play an important role in adjustment to urban life. An obvious hypothesis is that involvement in an extended kinship system makes it more difficult for Indian nuclear families to move to, and adjust to, urban environments. Presumably the kin network on the reservation or in the rural community constantly exerts pressure on individuals to remain in, or return to, the traditional locale. But the little evidence that does exist suggests that the process is not so simple. The extended family may exert pressure in both directions, it seems.

William Hodge describes the migration history of a Navajo man, Walter Higgins, in "Navajo Urban Migration: An Analysis from the Perspective of the Family" [90]. Noting that their traditional culture warns Navajos to "be wary of nonrelatives," Hodge describes the role of Higgins's nine siblings and other relatives in his history of moving away from and back to the Navajo reservations. Higgins has relatives who have moved off the reservation (some, into cities) and others who have not. Although many of his relatives have never lived off the reservation and many others have left only to return, one brother has earned a degree in civil engineering from the University of Denver and is head of a drafting department in a steel fabrication company in Dallas. Hodge argues that Higgins's case is not unique. Indian nuclear families tend to be relatively large, and the extended family includes many individuals. Thus, any Indian in the traditional locale is likely to have relatives who are already "urbanized." There is no a priori reason to assume these relatives will have less influence than ones that have never left the traditional locale. The importance American Indians attach to kinship might, at least in the short run, therefore, ease the transition to urban life for many individuals.

Research by John G. Red Horse and others entitled "Family Behavior of Urban American Indians" [140] illustrates another way kinship may promote rural-to-urban transition. The extended families of American Indians appear to persist in urban settings, since Red Horse and his colleagues observe that the Indian functional family in the city consists of several individual-household nuclear families providing support for one another. Thus, at least in larger cities with substantial American Indian populations, recent immigrants tend not to sever ties with extended family members; rather, they simply exchange one set of relatives for another. Probable exceptions to this, however, are those American Indian migrants who marry non-Indians. (Two articles that examine this pattern of marriage are by Burma [19] and Wagner [185].) Robert E. Ritzenthaler and Mary Sellers in "Indians in an Urban Situation" [142], identified another pattern among Indians in Milwaukee, however: urban residence afforded greater opportunity to meet potential marriage partners from reservations other than one's own.

Although urban kinship networks can provide emotional, social, and economic support in the short run, it is possible that longer-term consequences are in fact dysfunctional for an individual's adjustment to the city. If the extended kin groups promote (traditional) values and behavior inconsistent with the demands of an urban industrial system, then individuals involved in these kinship systems might have more difficulty in the long run adjusting to the new environment. Red Horse's research provides tentative evidence that this is not the case, however. Extended kin groups vary widely in the extent to which they combine traditional Indian culture with urban culture. While some groups do attempt to adhere strictly to traditional life-styles (as much as possible in an urban area), other groups become "bicultural" and retain some traditional patterns as well as adopting those of the urban place. To the extent that this occurs, an individual moving to the city will experience a unique social system "between two worlds" to ease the transition.

The extended family in the urban locale may also contribute to individuals in other ways. Carolyn L. Attneave, for example, in "Therapy in Tribal Settings and Urban Network Intervention" [4], describes what she calls the "method of network therapy" to assist Indians in coping with new urban environments. The method mobilizes relatives and friends to aid individuals in overcoming particular crises.

While the research summarized above emphasizes functional contributions of the urban kin network, the kinship system left behind in the traditional locale must also be considered. In his study of the Oneida Indian community in Wisconsin, "A 'Rural' Indian Community in an Urban Setting" [45], John H. Dowling notes extensive visiting between members of the community and individuals who have moved as far away as Milwaukee and Chicago. The urban individual returns regularly for week-end visits and thus never really severs ties with his traditional community. Furthermore, many who have emigrated return in their later years to communities of origin. Although this might not appear on the surface to work against adjustment to urban life, a desire to return frequently to a previous locale limits geographical mobility in most instances. To visit the Oneida community regularly from Milwaukee is quite different from making regular visits from New York, for example. In other words, ties with kin generally can be maintained only if one does not move very far from one's traditional community, and this may not necessarily give access to the city providing the best opportunities. Additionally, "to adjust to urban life" generally means more than adapting to one specific city. Urban industrial society frequently requires individuals, Indian and non-Indian, to move several times to where jobs are situated. Thus an American Indian who has moved from the Oneida community to Milwaukee might have to take another step to an even more distant place if economic opportunities deteriorate in Milwaukee or greater ones develop in another city.

It is thus very often impossible to live successfully in two worlds, and the advantages of one or the other must often be sacrificed. Stuart Jamieson [96] describes how trade unions created this bind for native Americans at Vancouver, British Columbia. Hundreds who once moved from longshore work to fishing and back had by midcentury been reduced to only seventy-two by a rule that put those leaving at the bottom of the seniority list on their return.

Two anthropologists analyzing American Indian urbanization from a regional ecological perspective have, however, identified a kind of city where migrants can live successfully in two worlds. Hodge [90] labels smaller cities such as Shiprock, New Mexico, as "transitional" between Navajo reservation camps and metropolitan Albuquerque. More recently, J. Anthony Paredes, in "Chippewa Townspeople" [132], describes how Anishinabes (Ojibwas or Chippewas) in a small city near various Minnesota reservations enjoy the material benefits of urban employment and housing combined with continued participation in reservation social events and kin networks. Many Anishinabes moved to this small city after initially migrating to larger cities farther from the reservations.

While the studies cited above focus on the interplay between the extended family and urbanism, two studies raise issues related to the American Indian *nuclear* family in an urban environment. One of these is a comparison of Navajo and White mothers' evaluations of the behavior of children. George Michael Guilmet's study "Maternal Perceptions of Urban Navajo and Caucasian Children's Classroom Behavior" [73] suggests that while White mothers consider verbal, physically active children to be intelligent and well socialized, Navajo mothers generally consider such behavior rude and a result of improper socialization. Ann Metcalf's "From Schoolgirl to Mother: The Effects of Education on Navajo Women" [121] is a study of Navajo women in urban areas who were forced off their reservations as children and placed in boarding schools. The findings suggest that this experience adversely affected the women and produced low self-esteem and negative opinions of themselves as mothers. They also suggest that these women's children—the first generation of city-born Navajos—have adjustment problems linked to their mothers' experiences.

These two studies imply that the conflict between American Indian cultures and non-Indian contemporary urban ones will also be experienced by Indians born in cities. Whether this conflict will vanish after several generations of urban residence, as it seems to have done in other racial and ethnic groups, is an unanswered question. An important factor is likely to be whether city-born Indians develop attachments to traditional lands and locales during childhood. To the extent that their parents maintain close ties with nonurban Indians, it is more likely that children will develop such ties.

In addition to the research discussed above, three books devote some attention to urbanization and the American Indian family. In their classic work *The Navajo* [103], first published in 1947, Clyde Kluckhohn and Dorothea Leighton anticipated some of the problems American Indians would have in adapting to an urban, industrial society. Two other, less well known monographs are Edgar J. Dosman's *Indians: The Urban Dilemma* [44]; and Barbara C. Smucker's *Wigwam in the City* [153].

Finally, several theses and dissertations have examined issues pertaining to the urban Indian family. These works include Clara B. Cowan's "Assimilation of the Cherokees as Revealed in a Hundred Urban Families" [36]; Billye Y. Sherman Fogleman's "Adaptive Mechanisms of the North American Indian to an Urban Setting" [55]; Jeanne E. Guillemin's "The Micmac Indians in Boston: The Ethnography of an Urban Community" [70]; Thomas Eugene Glass's "A Descriptive and Comparative Study of American Children in the Detroit Public Schools" [59]; Robert Dale McCracken's "Urban Migration and the Changing Structure of Navajo Social Relations" [116]; Romola McSwain's "The Role of Wives in the Urban Adjustment of Navajo Migrant Families to Denver, Colorado" [118]; and George Michael Guilmet's "The Nonverbal American Indian Child in the Urban Classroom" [72].

Alcohol Consumption, Crime, and Mental Health

Alcohol Consumption

Here we report an argument found in recent research on drinking and alcoholism: that patterns of alcohol consumption among urban American Indians should be viewed within the context of the role of alcohol in traditional American Indian communities, since different cultures attach different meanings to alcohol consumption and intoxication. The argument suggests further that a large number of American Indians do not view heavy drinking (or even alcoholism) as a "problem" in their traditional communities, and that they bring this view of alcohol consumption with them to urban settings.

It has been documented that fairly extensive drinking often occurs in traditional Indian communities (see Littman [113]). Urban Indians may also be heavy users of alcohol: for example, Littman indicates that nearly half of the Navajo migrants to Denver are arrested at least once for alcohol-related offenses; and Edward P. Dozier [46] estimates that arrests for alcohol-related crimes among Indians are twelve times the national average.

Although various tribes have laws prohibiting or restricting the sale of alcohol on reservations, and though various messianic movements (e.g., the Ghost Dances, Handsome Lake) have emphasized the "evils" of alcohol, observers tend to agree that in traditional Indian communities extensive drinking does not generally carry the same stigma as it does among most Whites.

Although there is no direct evidence, it seems reasonable to assume that Indians tend to bring this view (to the extent it exists) when they move to urban settings. A study at least relevant is Herbert Locklear's "American Indian Alcoholism" [114], a report of a survey indicating that American Indians in Baltimore do not perceive their community as having an "alcohol problem," though their rate of alcoholism is twice that of the White population in Baltimore.

The relative lack of social constraints is perceived as only one feature of American Indian drinking, however. Another is the strongly group-oriented nature of alcohol consumption. In a paper mentioned above, Dozier [46] argues that the stereotypical alcoholic, as a person who attempts to hide his alcohol dependence from friends and relatives, is very rare among American Indians. On the contrary, he argues, most regular, heavy drinking by American Indians is done among friends and relatives.

The questions "why" social constraints may be weak and "why" heavy drinking seems to be primarily group behavior in traditional communities are beyond the scope of this bibliographical essay. (Both Littman and Dozier link these patterns to historical Indian-White relations.) However, three studies of the use of alcohol in urban settings may be better understood using this view.

Two of the studies are by Frances Northend Ferguson and involve data from an alcohol treatment center in Gallup, New Mexico. They compare drinking behavior of Navajos who are integrated exclusively into their traditional culture with that of Navajos attempting to adapt to an urban environment. In the first study, "Navajo Drinking: Some Tentative Hypotheses" [50], Ferguson argues there are two types of heavy drinkers: "recreation drinkers" and "anxiety drinkers." The former, the traditional type of Indian heavy drinker, drink for entertainment and are strongly attached to their traditional culture, generally avoiding urban, industrial society. The latter, on the other hand, are less involved in traditional Navajo society and are employed in various modern, urban occupations.

One might suspect the "anxiety drinkers" to respond more favorably to conventional treatment programs than the "recreation drinkers," who are more closely linked to a culture in which such behavior is not so deviant. This was not the finding, however. Instead, treatment efforts were more successful for "recreation drinkers" than for "anxiety drinkers." This apparent anomaly is "explained" by suggesting that the extra stress of high aspirations and limited resources for realizing them, characteristic of many Indians in cities, produces more acute alcohol problems. Though alcoholism may be a problem for many traditional and many urban Indians, it is more severe for urban Indians because of the unique stress they experience, asserts Ferguson.

In "Stake Theory as an Explanatory Device in

Navajo Alcoholism Treatment Response" [51], Ferguson develops a more sophisticated theory. Here Navajo males are classified as "having a stake" primarily in their traditional culture; primarily in modern culture; or primarily in neither, but divided between the two. Those with "stakes" primarily in modern culture were least responsive to treatment for alcoholism, and it was argued this was because their "stake" was incomplete. Although they had jobs in the modern economy, this involvement did not extend into other realms of participation, leading to complete integration into urban life. Involvement in the larger society ended when the workday ended: in the evening and on weekends the men sought the companionship of fellow tribesmen in the city. In these settings, argues Ferguson, a form of traditional behavior is readily available—group drinking. Thus, according to Ferguson, drinking is a means whereby one may bridge the gap between White and Indian worlds. (Some of this, however may be unique to Gallup, New Mexico, since that city seems to offer American Indians few if any other forms of recreation. See Leonard McCombe with Evon Z. Vogt and Clyde Kluckhohn, *Navaho Means People* [115], for a photographic study of Navajos in Gallup, enabling one to see the sociocultural context of alcohol consumption there.)

This line of reasoning found in the literature culminates in "For Individual Power and Social Credit: The Use of Alcohol among Tucson Papagos" [182], by Jack O. Waddell. From interviews with Indian males in

Tucson, Waddell concludes that intoxication might have an important (positive) function for urban Indians. Noting that most Indian cultures devalue individual "success" that does not contribute to the group, Waddell argues that individual economic success may be a stigma for urban Indians. "Shared drunkenness" may become a mechanism whereby status differences are lessened, since it is a way for one successful in the larger society to demonstrate to fellow Indians that he is still "Indian."

There is, nevertheless, no definitive evidence in the literature to support this argument. It is clear, however, that if the argument is correct (and we are not sure it is), then there are complex policy issues surrounding the "problem" of Indian drinking. In an extreme case, to "treat" drinking behavior of urban Indians while not providing alternative opportunities for traditional behavior may deprive them of a source of Indian identity. It may be for this reason that Indian-controlled alcoholic treatment programs may prove more effective than non-Indian-controlled ones.

There are also other published works considering urban Indian drinking, including Theodore D. Graves's "Acculturation, Access and Alcohol in a Tri-Ethnic Community" [62]; Dwight B. Heath's "Prohibition and Post-Repeal Drinking Patterns among the Navajo" [83]; John J. and Irma Honigmann's "Drinking in an Indian-White Community" [93]; Wesley R. Hurt, Jr., and Richard M. Brown's "Social Drinking Patterns of the Yankton Sioux" [95]; Robert E. Kutter and Albert

B. Lorincz's "Alcoholism and Addiction in Urbanized Sioux Indians" [104]; Michael W. Everett and Jack O. Waddell's *Native American Drinking in the Southwest* [49]; and Jerrold E. Levy and Stephen J. Kunitz's *Indian Drinking: Navajo Practices and Anglo-American Theories* [110]. Finally, two dissertations consider this issue: "Adaptive Strategies of Urban Indian Drinkers," by Gretchen Mary Chesley Lang [106]; and "Modernization and Symptoms of Stress: Attitudes, Accidents and Alcohol Use among Urban Papago Indiana" [163], by Donald David Stull. Also see Stull [164].

Crime

Whether or not high alcohol consumption is a problem in itself, it does lead to involvement with the criminal justice system. In "Crime, Delinquency, and the American Indian" [98], Gary F. Jensen, Joseph H. Stauss, and V. William Harris analyze Uniform Crime Reports and show that American Indians have a much higher arrest rate (in both rural and urban areas) than either Blacks or Whites. In urban areas in 1970, the arrest rate (per 100,000) was 27,535 for Indians, 7,715 for Blacks, and 2,423 for Whites. This extremely high rate for Indians is mostly due to alcohol-related offenses: the arrest rate in 1970 for this type of offense was 21,069 for Indians, 1,867 for Blacks, and 937 for Whites. A possible explanation is that police discriminate against American Indians in making arrests. However, Jensen and his colleagues challenge this as-

sumption using data from a study of self-reported delinquency among Anglo, Chicano, and American Indian youth in Arizona. A more likely explanation is
linked to the frequent group and public nature of Indian alcohol use, making their behavior under the
influence of alcohol more visible to police.

Three articles focus on problems American Indians have when confronting the unfamiliar White
criminal justice system in cities. These are "Confrontation with the Law: The Case of the American Indians
in Seattle" [22] by Bruce A. Chadwick, Joseph Stauss,
Howard M. Bahr, and Lowell K. Halverson; "The Indian Patrol in Minneapolis: Social Control and Social
Change in an Urban Context" [27] by Fay G. Cohen;
and "An Experimental Outreach Legal Aid Program
for an Urban Native American Population Utilizing
Legal Paraprofessionals" [160] by Joseph H. Stauss,
Bruce A. Chadwick, Howard M. Bahr, and Lowell K.
Halverson.

Other articles examine aspects of urban Indian
crime. They include David M. Brady's "Indian Juvenile
Delinquency—So Different?" [16]; Robert E. Kuttner
and Albert B. Lorincz's "Promiscuity and Prostitution
in Urbanized Indian Communities" [105]; Elizabeth
Eggleston's "Urban Indians in Criminal Courts" [48];
Morris A. Forslund and Virginia A. Cranston's "A
Self-Report Comparison of Indian and Anglo Delinquency in Wyoming" [56]; and Omer C. Stewart's
"Questions Regarding American Indian Criminality"
[162]. Also to be mentioned here is D. H. Swett's thesis

examining patterns of crime and deviance among American Indians in cities, "Deviant Behavior and Urban Adjustment: The American Indian Case in San Francisco and Oakland" [166].

Mental Health

There have also been studies of mental health (loosely defined) among urban American Indians. Some concern personality traits conducive to adjustment to urban life and are discussed in another section. Others describe the "mental health" of urban Indians and are discussed here.

A study by Luis S. Kemnitzer, "Adjustment and Value Conflict in Urbanizing Dakota Indians Measured by Q Sort Techniques" [100], is an intensive examination of nine Sioux Indians in San Francisco. He concludes that these Sioux must frequently behave in ways inconsistent with their own self-concepts because of conflict between the values of urban society and those of traditional Sioux society. A study by Daniel J. Reschly and F. J. Jipson entitled "Ethnicity, Geographic Locale, Age, Sex and Urban-Rural Residence as Variables in the Prevalence of Mild Retardation" [141] considers the relationships between mild and severe retardation and both ethnicity and urban-rural residence. The results suggest that mild, but not severe, retardation is more prevalent among American Indians than among Whites, and that urban or rural residence makes no difference in this regard.

Other work on the mental health of urban American Indians includes Theodore D. Graves's "The Navajo Urban Migrant and His Psychological Situation" [65]; Jeraldine S. Withycombe's "Relationships of Self-Concept, Social Status, and Self-Perceived Social Status and Racial Differences of Paiute Indian and White Elementary School Children" [195]; Alfred M. Braxton's "Blood Pressure Changes among Male Navajo Migrants to an Urban Environment" [17]; Trevor Denton's "Canadian Indian Migrants and Impression Management of Ethnic Stigma" [41]; and Stanley Sue, David B. Allen, and Linda Conaway's "The Responsiveness and Equality of Mental Health Care to Chicanos and Native Americans" [165]. A relevant thesis and dissertation are Richard Frost's "A Study of a Los Angeles Urban Indian Free Clinic and Indian Mental Problems" [58]; and Craig Ernest Henrikson's "Acculturation, Value Change and Mental Health among the Navajo" [86].

Perhaps because so much attention has been devoted to alcoholism, the question of urban American Indian mental health is thus neglected in the research literature. Certainly more work could be done on the psychological consequences of American Indian urban migration.

Continued Urbanization: Assimilation and Adaptation

There is probably agreement among Indians and Whites as to the importance of improving many conditions of American Indian life. Undoubtedly, most members of both groups would like to see Indians raise their income levels, attain better jobs, have improved health care, and experience expanded educational opportunities. However, as Howard M. Bahr and Bruce A. Chadwick point out in "Conservatism, Racial Intolerance, and Attitudes toward Racial Assimilation among Whites and American Indians" [6], there is often considerable disagreement when it comes to actually accomplishing these worthwhile objectives.

Considerable prejudice against American Indians still exists among other members of American society, as discussed by Howard M. Bahr, Bruce A. Chadwick, and Joseph Stauss in "Discrimination against Urban Indians in Seattle" [7]. This prejudice is reflected in employment in many (if not all) urban areas, as illustrated by Joan Ablon in "Retention of Cultural Values and Differential Urban Adaptation: Samoans and American Indians in a West Coast City" [3]. On the other hand, however, many American Indians themselves feel what Ablon, in "Relocated American Indians in the San Francisco Bay Area: Social Interactions and Indian Identity" [1], refers to as a basic antagonism toward White society. As a consequence, many American Indians refuse to establish non-Indian contacts with mainstream urban American society.

Given agreement on the need to improve social, economic, and physical conditions for American Indians, but also given opposition on the part of many Whites and Indians to full Indian assimilation into larger society, what are the alternatives? In a previously mentioned paper, Sol Tax [168] argues that most American Indians do not actually want to be part of mainstream society and that socioeconomic opportunities should be improved without requiring them to relinquish Indian identities. These identities typically rest on fundamental differences between Indians and Whites. Ablon [1] also argues this, as do J. Milton Yinger and George Eaton Simpson in "The Integration of Americans of Indian Descent" [197].

There are, of course, different kinds (and degrees) of assimilation other than total submersion. Yinger and Simpson outline four: (1) amalgamation, that is, biological intermixture through intermarriage; (2) psychological identification, that is, sharing cognitive and emotional patterns; (3) acculturation or cultural assimilation, that is, mixing or blending of different cultures; and (4) structural assimilation, that is, integration at the primary group level. They suggest that while total assimilation of American Indians into larger society may be a realizable ideal, some form of pluralism is likely to continue for some time. In "Urbanizaton, Peoplehood and Modes of Identity: Native Americans in Cities" [161], James H. Stewart argues that many American Indians in urban areas are consciously pluralistic and adopt an approach of "strategic culturalism"; that is, they maintain two identities, one in the White world, another in the Indian world.

Extensive research has been conducted on *determinants* of assimilation or adjustment of American Indians to urban society. Specific findings of this research are shown in the following five studies. In "The Assimilation of American Indians into Urban Society: The Seattle Case" [21], Bruce A. Chadwick and Joseph H. Stauss report that American Indians with small proportions of Indian ancestry and low levels of self-identification as Indians are more likely to adapt to life in Seattle and remain there. They also find that, though most Indians support assimilation as an eventual goal, the general level of assimilation in Seattle is low and that there is no correlation between assimilation and either length of time in Seattle or involvement with White friends. In his study, Price [137] reports that involvement in pan-Indian enclaves and associations promotes adjustment to life in Los Angeles. Martin [120] indicates that Indians who possess small proportions of Indian blood, are younger, and have a background of both public and BIA schools are more likely to adjust successfully to the urban environment. Weppner [191] indicates that married Indians and those able to speak English well are more likely to adapt and adjust to urban life. Yinger and Simpson [197] argue that urbanization, education, improved economic conditions, and intermarriage all contribute to adjustment and to eventual assimilation of American Indians in American society

Other research on assimilation includes Howard M. Bahr and Bruce A. Chadwick's "Contemporary Perspectives on Indian Americans: A Review Essay" [5]; William C. Cockerham and Audie L. Blevins, Jr.'s,

"Open School vs. Traditional School: Self-Identification among Native American and White Adolescents" [26]; Edward P. Dozier, George Simpson, and J. Milton Yinger's "The Integration of Americans of Indian Descent" [47]; Theodore D. Graves's "Psychological Acculturation in a Tri-Ethnic Community" [63]; James Hirabayashi, William Willard, and Luis S. Kemnitzer's "Pan-Indianism in the Urban Setting" [87]; Alexander Lesser's "Education and the Future of Tribalism in the United States: The Case of the American Indian" [109]; Robert K. Thomas's "Pan-Indianism" [169]; and Joseph H. Stauss and Bruce A. Chadwick's "Urban Indian Adjustment" [159].

Summary and Conclusions

Based on the review and analysis of research presented here, the recent urbanization of American Indians may be viewed as processes of *cultural, social,* and *economic change.* Anthropological and historical research presented in an earlier section indicates that native peoples of the Western Hemisphere have lived for centuries in cities and quasi-urban communities. Modern urbanization began in the late 1940s and early 1950s and will likely continue for some time. Many *cultural changes* involved in this recent urbanization actually began before movement to urban areas. Through the mass media and educational institutions, American Indians surely began to absorb norms and values of an increasingly urban American society. As they moved to urban areas, they often discovered that behavior viewed as normal and admirable in tribal settings—for example, quietness and unaggressiveness, was considered odd (even pathological) by White society. Faced with such conflicts between traditional and urban ways, individual Indians were often forced to adjust culturally in ways ranging from total assimilation to cultural pluralism. The failure to do so sometimes resulted in alcoholism and crime. Similar adjustments on a group level have resulted in such phenomena as urban pan-Indian movements and pan-Indian dances, powwows, and similar gatherings.

Social changes involved in urbanization include a diminished role for extended families and a lessening of tribal importance. Though many American Indians continue to maintain extended family ties after moving to urban areas, the ties are typically no longer as pervasive as they were on reservations and in rural areas. Urbanization has also weakened the tribes themselves by moving members out of tribal areas and by replacing tribal functions with those of other urban organizations. On the other hand, however, urbanization seems to have produced a heightened sense of social awareness and has provided an arena for increasing pan-Indian activism.

Whether urbanization will be viewed as a positive force among contemporary Indian peoples may depend largely on its effect on *economic conditions*. Research indicates that American Indians move to urban areas primarily to improve their economic situations, either through better jobs or through access to better organized or better quality services. Research also indicates that urbanization can be a successful means of "upward mobility" for young, educated Indian males with training and experience. Rural-to-urban migration will probably continue to improve the economic conditions of Indians who choose to migrate in the decades ahead.

Though it is difficult to select a single factor as *most* important in facilitating these processes of cultural, social, and economic change, work is a very important one—perhaps *the* most important. In contemporary American society, work provides two major "rewards" for most people: a salary or wage, and the principal component of an individual's identity. It is through a job that most individuals receive money, and it is through a job in an urban area that most American Indians are able to improve their economic situation. Most White American males also think of themselves largely as members of some occupational group. Though this definition of identity may be alien to traditional Indian people, their adoption of this view seems responsible for many of the changes discussed above.

ALPHABETICAL LIST AND INDEX

*Denotes items suitable for secondary school students

spectives on Indian Americans: A Review Essay." *Social Science Quarterly* 53:606–18. (50)

[6] ———. 1974. "Conservatism, Racial Intolerance, and Attitudes toward Racial Assimilation among Whites and American Indians." *Journal of Social Psychology* 94:45–56. (48)

*[7] Bahr, Howard M., Bruce A. Chadwick, and Joseph Stauss. 1972. "Discrimination against Urban Indians in Seattle." *Indian Historian* 5:4–11. (48)

[8] Baumhoff, Martin A. 1958. "California Athabascan Groups." *University of California Anthropological Records* 16:157–237. (11)

[9] Bauxar, J. Joseph. 1978. "History of the Illinois Area." In *Handbook of North American Indians,* vol. 15, *Northeast,* ed. Bruce G. Trigger, 594–601. Washington, D.C.: Smithsonian Institution, Government Printing Office. (8)

[10] Beale, Calvin L. 1973. "Migration Patterns of Minorities in the United States." *American Journal of Agricultural Economics* 55:938–46. (4, 13, 20)

[11]   Bee, Robert L. 1969. "Tribal Leadership in the War on Poverty: A Case Study." *Social Science Quarterly* 50:676–86.   (27)

[12]   Bee, Robert L., and R. Gingerich, 1971. "Colonialism, Classes, and Ethnic Identity: Native Americans and the National Political Economy." *Studies in Comparative National Development* 12:70–93.   (31)

[13]   Bigony, Beatrice Anne. 1974. "Migrants to the City: A Study of the Subeconomic Status of Native Americans in Detroit and Michigan." Ph.D diss., University of Michigan.   (29)

[14]   Bloom, Joseph D. 1973. "Migration and Psychopathology of Eskimo Women." *American Journal of Psychiatry* 130:446–49.   (20)

[15]   Blumenfeld, Ruth. 1965. "Mohawks: Round Trip to the High Steel." *Transaction* 3:19–22.   (23)

*[16] Brady, David M., Sr. 1967. "Indian Juvenile Delinquency—So Different?" *Journal of American Indian Education* 6:23–25.   (45)

[17] Braxton, Alfred M. 1970. "Blood Pressure Changes among Male Navaho Migrants to an Urban Environment." *Canadian Review of Sociology and Anthropology* 7:189–200. (47)

[18] Breton, Raymond, and Gail Grant Akian. n.d. *Urban Institutions and People of Indian Ancestry.* Occasional Paper no. 5. Halifax South, Nova Scotia: Institute for Research on Public Policy. (23)

[19] Burma, John H. 1963. "Interethnic Marriage in Los Angeles, 1948–59." *Social Forces* 42:156–65. (26, 33)

*[20] Catlin, George. 1841. *Letters and Notes on the Manners, Customs, and Conditions of the North American Indians.* New York: Wiley and Putnam. Published the same year in London by the author. Reprinted in many editions. Most accessible, New York: Dover, 1971. (3, 9)

[21] Chadwick, Bruce A., and Joseph H. Stauss. 1975. "The Assimilation of American Indians into Urban Society: The Seattle Case." *Human Organization* 34:359–69. (50)

[22]   Chadwick, Bruce A., Joseph Stauss, Howard M. Bahr, and Lowell K. Halverson. 1976. "Confrontation with the Law: The Case of the American Indians in Seattle." *Phylon* 37:163–71.   (45)

[23]   Chadwick, Bruce A., and Lynn C. White. 1973. "Correlates of Length of Urban Residence among the Spokane Indians." *Human Organization* 32:9–16.   (21)

[24]   Clinton, Lawrence, Bruce A. Chadwick, and Howard M. Bahr. 1973. "Vocational Training for Indian Migrants: Correlates of 'Success' in a Federal Program." *Human Organization* 32:17–27.   (30)

[25]   ———. 1975. "Urban Relocation Reconsidered: Antecedents of Employment among Indian Males." *Rural Sociology* 40:117–33.   (28)

[26]   Cockerham, William C., and Audie L. Blevins, Jr. 1976. "Open School vs. Traditional School: Self-Identification among Native American and White Adolescents." *Sociology of Education* 49:164–69.   (51)

*[27]   Cohen, Fay G. 1973. "The Indian Patrol in Minneapolis: Social Control and

Social Change in an Urban Context."
Law and Society Review 7:779–86.   (45)

[28]   Cook, Sherburne F. 1943. "Migration
       and Urbanization of the Indians in
       California." *Human Biology* 15:33–45.   (3)

[29]   ———. 1955. "The Aboriginal Popula-
       tion of the San Joaquin Valley,
       California." *University of California Publi-
       cations, Anthropological Records* 16:31–78.   (11)

[30]   ———. 1956. "The Aboriginal Popula-
       tion of the North Coast of California."
       *University of California Publications An-
       thropological Records* 16:81–129.   (11)

[31]   ———. 1957. "The Aboriginal Popula-
       tion of Alameda and Contra Costa
       Counties, California." *University of
       California Publications, Anthropological
       Records* 16:131–55.   (11)

[32]   ———. 1960. "Colonial Expeditions to
       the Interior of California, Central Val-
       ley, 1800–1820." *University of California
       Publications, Anthropological Records*
       16:239–92.   (11)

*[33] ———. 1976. *The Conflict between the
       California Indian and White Civilization.*

Berkeley: University of California
Press.   (3)

[34] ———. 1976. *The Indian Population of
New England in the Seventeenth Century*.
Berkeley: University of California
Press.   (9)

[35] ——— 1976. *The Population of the
California Indians, 1769–1970*. Berkeley: University of California Press.   (3, 11)

[36] Cowan, Clara B. 1941. "Assimilation of
the Cherokees as Revealed in a
Hundred Urban Families." Master's
thesis, University of Missouri.   (38)

[37] Culbert, T. Patrick. 1974. *The Lost
Civilization: The Story of the Classic Maya*.
New York: Harper and Row.   (7)

[38] ———. 1978. "Mesoamerica." In *Ancient Native Americans*, ed. Jesse D. Jennings, pp. 403–53. San Francisco: W.
H. Freeman.   (7)

[39] Davis, Kingsley. 1955. "The Origin and
Growth of Urbanization in the World."
American Journal of Sociology 60:429–37. (1, 2)

[40]   Denton, Trevor. 1972. "Migration from a Canadian Indian Reserve." *Journal of Canadian Studies* 7:54–62.   (23)

[41]   ———. 1975. "Canadian Indian Migrants and Impression Management of Ethnic Stigma." *Canadian Review of Sociology and Anthropology* 12:65–71.   (47)

*[42]   Dobyns, Henry F. 1976. *Native American Historical Demography: A Critical Bibliography.* Bloomington: Indiana University Press.   (3)

[43]   ———. 1976. *Spanish Colonial Tucson: A Demographic History.* Tucson: University of Arizona Press.   (3)

[44]   Dosman, Edgar J. 1972. *Indians: The Urban Dilemma.* Toronto: McClelland and Stewart.   (38)

[45]   Dowling, John H. 1968. "A 'Rural' Indian Community in an Urban Setting." *Human Organization* 27:236–39.   (35)

[46]   Dozier, Edward P. 1966. "Problem Drinking among American Indians: The Role of Socio-Cultural Depriva-

tion." *Quarterly Journal of Studies of Alcohol* 27:72– 87.   (39, 40)

[47]   Dozier, Edward P., George E. Simpson, and J. Milton Yinger. 1957. "The Integration of Americans of Indian Descent." *Annals of the American Academy of Political and Social Science* 311:158– 65.   (51)

[48]   Eggleston, Elizabeth. 1976. "Urban Indians in Criminal Courts." *University of Western Australia Law Review* 12:368– 404.   (45)

[49]   Everett, Michael W., and Jack O. Waddell, eds. 1980. *Native American Drinking in the Southwest.* Tucson: University of Arizona Press.   (44)

[50]   Ferguson, Frances Northend. 1968. "Navajo Drinking: Some Tentative Hypotheses." *Human Organization* 27:159– 67.   (41)

[51]   ——— . 1976. "Stake Theory as an Explanatory Device in Navajo Alcoholism Treatment Response." *Human Organization* 35:65– 78.   (42)

[52]   Flad, Harvey. 1972. "The Urban American Indians of Syracuse, New York:

Human Exploration of Urban Ethnic Space." *Antipode* 4:88–99.   (26)

[53]   ———. 1973. "The City and the Longhouse: A Social Geography of American Indians in Syracuse, New York." Ph.D. diss., Syracuse University.   (26)

*[54]   Fogelson, Raymond D. 1978. *The Cherokees: A Critical Bibliography.* Bloomington: Indiana University Press.   (10)

[55]   Fogleman, Billye Y. Sherman. 1972. "Adaptive Mechanisms of the North American Indian to an Urban Setting." Ph.D. diss., Southern Methodist University.   (38)

[56]   Forslund, Morris A., and Virgina A. Cranston. 1975. "A Self-Report Comparison of Indian and Anglo Delinquency in Wyoming." *Criminology* 13:193–98.   (45)

*[57]   Fowler, Melvin L. 1975. "A Pre-Columbian Urban Center on the Mississippi." *Scientific American* 233:92–101.   (2, 8)

[58]   Frost, Richard. 1973. "A Study of a Los Angeles Urban Indian Free Clinic and

Indian Mental Problems." Master's thesis, California State University at Long Beach.   (47)

[59]   Glass, Thomas Eugene. 1972. "A Descriptive and Comparative Study of American Indian Children in the Detroit Public Schools." Ph.D diss., Wayne State University.   (38)

*[60]   Goodwin, Gary C. 1977. *Cherokees in Transition: A Study of Changing Culture and Environment prior to 1775.* Chicago: Department of Geography, University of Chicago.   (10)

[61]   Graves, Theodore D. 1966. "Alternative Models for the Study of Urban Migration." *Human Organization* 25:295–99.   (18)

[62]   ———. 1967. "Acculturation, Access and Alcohol in a Tri-Ethnic Community." *American Anthropologist* 69:306–21.   (43)

[63]   ———. 1967. "Psychological Acculturation in a Tri-Ethnic Community." *Southwestern Journal of Anthropology* 23:337–50.   (51)

[64] ———. 1970. "The Personal Adjustment of Navajo Indian Migrants to Denver, Colorado." *American Anthropologist* 72:35–54. (20)

[65] ———. 1973. "The Navajo Urban Migrant and His Psychological Situation." *Ethos,* pp. 321–24. (47)

[66] ———. 1974. "Urban Indian Personality and the 'Culture of Poverty.'" *American Ethnologist* 1:65–86. (30)

[67] Graves, Theodore D., and Charles A. Lave. 1972. "Determinants of Urban Migrant Indian Wages." *Human Organization* 31:47–61. (29)

[68] Graves, Theodore D., and Minor van Arsdale. 1966. "Values, Expectations and Relocation: The Navajo Migrant to Denver." *Human Organization* 25:301–7. (21)

[69] Griffin, James B. 1978. "The Midlands and Northeastern United States." In *Ancient Native Americans,* ed. Jesse D., Jennings, pp. 221–80. San Francisco: W. H. Freeman. (8)

[70] Guillemin, Jeanne E. 1973. "The Micmac Indians in Boston: The Ethnog-

raphy of an Urban Community." Ph.D.
diss., Brandeis University.   (38)

*[71]   ———. 1975. *Urban Renegades: The Cul-
tural Strategy of American Indians*. New
York: Columbia University Press.   (15)

[72]   Guilmet, George Michael. 1976. "The
Nonverbal American Indian Child in
the Urban Classroom." Ph.D diss., University of California.   (38)

[73]   ———. 1979. "Maternal Perceptions of
Urban Navajo and Caucasian Chil-
dren's Classroom Behavior." *Human
Organization* 38:87–91.   (37)

[74]   Gundlach, James H., and Alden E.
Roberts. 1978. "Native American Indian Migration and Relocation: Success
or Failure." *Pacific Sociological Review*
21:117–28.   (28)

*[75]   Gunther, Erna. 1972. *Indian Life on the
Northwest Coast of North America as Seen
by the Early Explorers and Fur Traders during the Last Decades of the Eighteenth Century*. Chicago: University of Chicago
Press.   (12)

[76] Hackenberg, Robert A. 1976. "Colorado River Basin Development and Its Potential Impact on Tribal life." *Human Organization* 35:303–11.   (31)

[77] Hackenberg, Robert A., and Mary M. Gallagher. 1972. "The Costs of Cultural Change: Accidental Injury and Modernization among the Papago Indians." *Human Organization* 31:211–26.   (25)

[78] Hackenberg, Robert A., and C. Roderick Wilson. 1972. "Reluctant Emigrants: The Role of Migration in Papago Indian Adaptation." *Human Organization* 31:171–86.   (30)

*[79] Hadley, J. Nixon. 1957. "The Demography of the American Indians." *Annals of the American Academy of Political and Social Science* 311:23–30.   (26)

*[80] Hardoy, Jorge E. 1964. *Pre-Columbian Cities*. New York: Walker.   (1, 2, 6)

[81] ———. 1968. *Urban Planning in Pre-Columbian America*. New York: George Braziller.   (6)

[82]   Harkins, Arthur M. 1971. *A Bibliogra-
        phy of Urban Indians in the United States*.
        Minneapolis: Center for Urban and
        Regional Affairs, University of Min-
        nesota.   (15)

[83]   Heath, Dwight B. 1964. "Prohibition
        and Post-Repeal Drinking Patterns
        among the Navajo." *Quarterly Journal of
        Studies on Alcohol* 25:119–35.   (43)

[84]   Heidenreich, Conrad E. 1978. "Hu-
        ron." In *Handbook of North American In-
        dians,* vol. 15, *Northeast,* ed. Bruce G.
        Trigger. Washington, D.C.: Smithso-
        nian Institution, Government Printing
        Office.   (9)

[85]   Heizer, Robert F., ed. 1978. *Handbook
        of North American Indians.* vol. 8.
        California. Washington, D.C.: Smithson-
        ian Institution, Government Printing
        Office.   (11)

[86]   Henrikson, Craig Ernest. 1971. "Accul-
        turation, Value Change and Mental
        Health among the Navajo." Ph.D. diss.,
        University of North Carolina.   (47)

[87]   Hirabayashi, James, William Willard,
        and Luis S. Kemnitzer. 1972. "Pan-

Indianism in the Urban Setting." In *The Anthropology of Urban Environments,* ed. Thomas Weaver and Douglas White, pp. 77–78. Society for Applied Anthropology Monograph no. 11. Washington: Society for Applied Anthropology. (51)

[88] Hodge, William. 1967. "Navaho Urban Silversmiths." *Anthropological Quarterly* 40:185–200. (20)

[89] ———. 1969. *The Albuquerque Navajos.* Tucson: University of Arizona Press. (15)

[90] ———. 1971. "Navajo Urban Migration: An Analysis from the Perspective of the Family." In *The American Indian in Urban Society*, ed. Jack O. Waddell and O. Michael Watson, pp. 346–91. Boston: Little, Brown. (32, 36)

[91] Hoffman, Bernard G. 1967. "Ancient Tribes Revisited: A Summary of Indian Distribution and Movement in the Northeastern United States from 1534 to 1779. Parts I–III." *Ethnohistory* 14:1–46. (9)

[92] Holden, David E. W. 1969. "Modernization among Town and Bush Cree in

Quebec." *Canadian Review of Sociology and Anthropology* 6:237–48.   (23)

[93]   Honigmann, John J., and Irma Honigmann. 1945. "Drinking in an Indian-White Community." *Quarterly Journal of Studies on Alcohol* 5:575–619.   (43)

[94]   Hurt, Wesley R., Jr. 1961. "The Urbanization of the Yankton Indians." *Human Organization* 20:226–31.   (22)

[95]   Hurt, Wesley R., Jr., and Richard M. Brown. 1965. "Social Drinking Patterns of the Yankton Sioux." *Human Organization* 24:222–30.   (43)

[96]   Jamieson, Stuart. 1961. "Native Indians and the Trade Union Movement in British Columbia." *Human Organization* 20:219–25.   (36)

[97]   Jennings, Jesse D., ed. 1978. *Ancient Native Americans.* San Francisco: W. H. Freeman.   (10)

[98]   Jensen, Gary F., Joseph H. Stauss, and V. William Harris. 1977. "Crime, Delinquency, and the American Indian." *Human Organization* 36:252–57.   (44)

[99] Jorgensen, Joseph G. 1978. "A Century of Political Economic Effects on American Indian Society, 1880–1980." *Journal of Ethnic Studies* 6:1–82.   (27)

[100] Kemnitzer, Luis S. 1973. "Adjustment and Value Conflict in Urbanizing Dakota Indians Measured by Q Sort Techniques." *American Anthropologist* 75:687–707.   (46)

[101] Kerri, James Nwannukwu. 1976. "'Push' and 'Pull' Factors: Reasons for Migration as a Factor in American Indian Urban Adjustment." *Human Organization* 35:215–20.   (19)

[102] King, Arden R. 1967. "Urbanization and Industrialization." In *Handbook of Middle American Indians*, ed. R. Wauchope, 6:512–36. Austin: University of Texas Press.   (23)

[103] Kluckhohn, Clyde, and Dorothea Leighton. 1974. *The Navajo.* New York: Doubleday.   (38)

[104] Kuttner, Robert E., and Albert B. Lorincz. 1967. "Alcoholism and Addic-

tion in Urbanized Sioux Indians." *Mental Hygiene* 51:530–42.   (44)

[105]   ———. 1970. "Promiscuity and Prostitution in Urbanized Indian Communities." *Mental Hygiene* 54:79–91.   (45)

[106]   Lang, Gretchen Mary Chesley. 1974. "Adaptive Strategies of Urban Indian Drinkers." Ph.D. diss., University of Missouri.   (44)

[107]   Lave, A. Charles, James V. Mueller, and Theodore D. Graves. 1978. "The Economic Payoff of Different Kinds of Education: A Study of Urban Migrants in Two Societies." *Human Organization* 37:157–62.   (30)

*[108]   League of Women Voters of Minnesota. 1974. *Indians in Minnesota*. Saint Paul: League of Women Voters of Minnesota.   (27)

[109]   Lesser, Alexander. 1961. "Education and the Future of Tribalism in the United States: The Case of the American Indian." *Social Service Review* 35:135–43.   (51)

[110]   Levy, Jerrold E., and Stephen J. Kunitz. 1974. *Indian Drinking: Navajo*

Practices and Anglo-American Theories.
New York: John Wiley. (44)

[111] Liberty, Margot, David V. Hughey, and Richard Scaglion. 1976. "Rural and Urban Omaha Indian Fertility." *Human Biology* 48:59–71. (24, 25)

[112] Lipe, William D. 1978. "The Southwest." In *Ancient Native Americans,* ed. Jesse D. Jennings, pp. 327–401. San Francisco: W. H. Freeman. (10)

[113] Littman, Gerard. 1970. "Alcoholism, Illness and Social Pathology among American Indians in Transition." *American Journal of Public Health* 60: 1769–87. (26, 39)

[114] Locklear, Herbert. 1977. "American Indian Alcoholism: Program for Treatment." *Social Work* 22:202–7. (40)

*[115] McCombe, Leonard (photographer), with Evon Z. Vogt and Clyde Kluckhohn. 1951. *Navaho Means People.* Cambridge: Harvard University Press. (42)

[116] McCracken, Robert Dale. 1968. "Urban Migration and the Changing Structure of Navajo Social Relations." Ph.D. diss., University of Colorado. (38)

[117]   MacNeish, Richard S. 1964. "The Origins of New World Civilization." *Scientific American* 211:29–37.   (7)

[118]   McSwain, Romola. 1965. "The Role of Wives in the Urban Adjustment of Navajo Migrant Families to Denver, Colorado." Master's thesis, University of Hawaii.   (38)

[119]   Margon, Arthur. 1976. "Indians and Immigrants: A Comparison of Groups New to the City." *Journal of Ethnic Studies* 4:17–28.   (16, 20)

[120]   Martin, Harry W. 1964. "Correlates of Adjustment among American Indians in an Urban Environment." *Human Organization* 23:290–95.   (21, 50)

[121]   Metcalf, Ann. 1976. "From Schoolgirl to Mother: The Effects of Education on Navajo Women." *Social Problems* 23:535–44.   (37)

*[122]   Millon, René. 1967. "Teotihuacán." *Scientific American* 216:38–48.   (7)

*[123]   Mooney, James. 1975. *Historical Sketch of the Cherokee.* Chicago: Aldine.   (3)

*[124]   Moseley, Michael E. 1975. "Chan chan: Andean Alternative of the Preindustrial City." *Science* 187:219–25.   (7)

[125]   ———. 1978. "The Evolution of Andean Civilization." In *Ancient Native Americans*, ed. Jesse D. Jennings, pp. 491–541. San Francisco: W. H. Freeman.   (7)

[126]   Muller, Jon D. 1978. "The Southeast." In *Ancient Native Americans,* ed. Jesse D. Jennings, pp. 281–325. San Francisco: W. H. Freeman.   (10)

*[127]   Neils, Elaine M. 1971. *Reservation to City: Indian Migration and Federal Relocation.* Chicago: University of Chicago Press.   (15)

[128]   Newberry Library Center for the History of the American Indian. 1981. *Urban Indians. Proceedings of the Third Annual Conference on Problems and Issues Concerning American Indians Today.* Chicago: Newberry Library.   (vii)

[129]   Officer, James E. 1971. "The American Indian and Federal Policy." In *The American Indian in Urban Society,* ed.

Jack O. Waddell and O. Michael Watson. Boston: Little, Brown.   (16)

[130] Ortiz, Alfonso, ed. 1979. *Handbook of North American Indians.* vol. 9. *Southwest.* Washington, D.C.: Smithsonian Institution, Government Printing Office.   (11)

[131] Panunzio, Constantine. 1942. "Intermarriage in Los Angeles, 1924–33." *American Journal of Sociology* 47:390–401.   (26)

[132] Paredes, J. Anthony. 1980. "Chippewa Townspeople." In *Anishinabe: Six Studies of Modern Chippewa,* ed. J. Anthony Paredes, pp. 324–96. Tallahassee: University Presses of Florida.   (36)

[133] Passel, Jeffrey S. 1976. "Provisional Evaluation of the 1970 Census Count of American Indians." *Demography* 13:397–409.   (24)

[134] Peck, John Gregory. 1972. "Urban Station—Migration of the Lumbee Indians." Ph.D. diss., University of North Carolina.   (20)

*[135] Pfeiffer, John. 1974. "America's First City." *Horizon* 16:58–63. (8)

*[136] ———. 1975. "The Life and Death of a Great City." *Horizon* 17:82–95. (7)

[137] Price, John A. 1968. "The Migration and Adaptation of American Indians to Los Angeles." *Human Organization* 27:168–75. (15, 19, 50)

[138] ———. 1975. "U.S. and Canadian Indian Urban Ethnic Institutions." *Urban Anthropology* 4:035–052. (20)

*[139] Prucha, Francis Paul, ed. 1975. *Documents of United States Indian Policy.* Lincoln: University of Nebraska Press. (16)

[140] Red Horse, John G., Ronald Lewis, Marvin Felt, and James Decker. 1978. "Family Behavior of Urban American Indians." *Social Casework* 59:67–72. (33)

[141] Reschly, Daniel J., and F. J. Jipson. 1976. "Ethnicity, Geographic Locale, Age, Sex and Urban-Rural Residence as Variables in the Prevalence of Mild Retardation." *American Journal of Mental Deficiency* 81:154–61. (46)

*[142]   Ritzenthaler, Robert, E. and Mary
         Sellers. 1955. "Indians in an Urban
         Situation." *Wisconsin Archeologist*, n.s.,
         36:147–61.   (34)

[143]   Romaniuk, A. 1974. "Modernization
         and Fertility: The Case of the James
         Bay Indians." *Canadian Review of Sociol-
         ogy and Anthropology* 11:344–59.   (25)

[144]   Romaniuk, A., and V. Piché. 1972.
         "Natality Estimates for the Canadian
         Indians by Stable Population Models,
         1900–1969." *Canadian Review of Sociol-
         ogy and Anthropology* 9:1–20.   (26)

*[145]   Ronda, James P., and James Axtell.
         1978. *Indian Missions: A Critical Bibliog-
         raphy.* Bloomington: Indiana University
         Press.   (3)

*[146]   Rosen, Lawrence S., and Kurt Gorwitz.
         1980. "New Attention to American In-
         dians." *American Demographics*, pp.
         18–25.   (24)

[147]   Roy, Prodipto. 1962. "The Measure-
         ment of Assimilation: The Spokane
         Indians." *American Journal of Sociology*
         67:541–51.   (22)

*[148] Schoolcraft, Henry R. 1975 [1846]. *Notes on the Iroquois; or, Contributions to the Statistics, Aboriginal History, Antiquities and General Ethnology of Western New York.* Millwood, N.Y.: Kraus Reprint Company. (9)

[149] Shannon, Lyle W. 1969. "The Economic Absorption and Cultural Integration of Immigrant Workers: Characteristics of the Individual versus the Nature of the System." *American Behavioral Scientist* 13:36–56. (31)

[150] Simmons, James L. 1977. "One Little, Two Little, Three Little Indians: Counting American Indians in Urban Society." *Human Organization* 36:76–79. (24)

*[151] Sjoberg, Gideon. 1965. *The Preindustrial City: Past and Present.* New York: Free Press. (1)

[152] Smith, Marian W., ed. 1949. *Indians of the Urban Northwest.* New York: Columbia University Press. (12)

[153] Smucker, Barbara C. 1966. *Wigwam in the City.* New York: E. P. Dutton. (38)

[154]   Snyder, Peter Z. 1973. "Social Interaction Patterns and Relative Urban Success: The Denver Navajo." *Urban Anthropology* 2:1–24.   (23)

[155]   Sorkin, Alan L. 1969. "Some Aspects of
American Indian Migration." *Social
Forces* 48:243–50.   (21, 31)

[156]   ———. 1978. "The Economic Basis of
Indian Life." *Annals of the American
Academy of Political and Social Science*
436:1–12.   (26)

[157]   ———. 1978. *The Urban American Indian*. Lexington, Mass.: Lexington
Books.   (13, 15)

*[158]   Stanley, Sam, and Robert K. Thomas.
1978. "Current Demographic and Social Trends among North American
Indians." *Annals of the American Academy
of Political and Social Science* 436:111–
20.   (19)

[159]   Stauss, Joseph H., and Bruce A.
Chadwick. 1979. "Urban Indian Ad-
justment." *American Indian Culture and
Research Journal* 3:23–38.   (51)

[160] Stauss, Joseph H., Bruce A. Chadwick, Howard M. Bahr, and Lowell K. Halverson. 1979. "An Experimental Outreach Legal Aid Program for an Urban Native American Population Utilizing Legal Paraprofessionals." *Human Organization* 38:386–94. (45)

[161] Stewart, James H. 1975. "Urbanization, Peoplehood and Modes of Identity: Native Americans in Cities." *Selected Proceedings of the First and Second Annual Conference on Minority Studies* 1:107–36. (49)

[162] Stewart, Omer C. 1964. "Questions Regarding American Indian Criminality." *Human Organization* 23:61–66. (45)

[163] Stull, Donald David. 1973. "Modernization and Symptoms of Stress: Attitudes, Accidents and Alcohol Use among Urban Papago Indians." Ph.D. diss., University of Colorado. (44)

[164] ———. 1977. "New Data on Accident Victim Rates among Papago Indians: The Urban Case." *Human Organization* 36:395–98. (44)

[165]   Sue, Stanley, David B. Allen, and Linda
        Conaway. 1978. "The Responsiveness
        and Equality of Mental Health Care to
        Chicanos and Native Americans." *Amer-
        ican Journal of Community Psychology*
        6:137–46.   (47)

[166]   Swett, D. H. 1965. "Deviant Behavior
        and Urban Adjustment: The American
        Indian Case in San Francisco and Oak-
        land." Master's thesis, San Francisco
        State College.   (46)

*[167] Task Force Eight: Urban and Rural
        Non-Reservation Indians. 1976. *Report
        on Urban and Rural Non-Reservation In-
        dians, Final Report to the American Indian
        Policy Review Commission*. Washington,
        D.C.: Government Printing Office.   (15)

*[168] Tax, Sol. 1978. "The Impact of Urbani-
        zation on American Indians." *Annals of
        the American Academy of Political and So-
        cial Science* 436:121–36.   (23, 49)

*[169] Thomas, Robert K. 1965. "Pan-
        Indianism." *Midcontinent American
        Studies Journal* 6:75–83.   (51)

*[170] Thornton, Russell, and Mary K. Gras-
        mick. 1980. *Sociology of American In-*

dians: A Critical Bibliography. Bloomington: Indiana University Press. (15)

[171] Thornton, Russell, and Joan Marsh-Thornton. 1981. "Estimating Prehistoric American Indian Population Size for the United States Area: Implications of the Nineteenth Century Populatin Decline and Nadir." *American Journal of Physical Anthropology* 55:47–53. (12)

*[172] Thwaites, Reuben Gold, ed. 1904–5. *Original Journals of the Lewis and Clark Expedition, 1804–1806.* 8 vols. New York: Dodd, Mead. Reprinted, New York: Arno, 1969. (12)

[173] Trigger, Bruce G., and James F. Pendergast. 1978. "Saint Lawrence Iroquoians." In *Handbook of North American Indians,* vol. 15, *Northeast,* ed. Bruce G. Trigger, pp. 357–61.Washington, D.C.: Smithsonian Institution, Government Printing Office. (9)

[174] Uhlmann, Julie M. 1972. "The Impact of Modernization on Papago Indian Fertility." *Human Organization* 31:149–62. (25)

*[175] United States Bureau of the Census. 1894. *The Five Civilized Tribes in Indian*

*Territory: The Cherokee, Chickasaw, Choc-
taw, Creek, and Seminole Nations.* Washington, D.C.: Census Printing Office.   (3)

[176]   ———. 1907. *Population of Oklahoma
and Indian Territory: 1907* Washington,
D.C.: Government Printing Office.   (3)

*[177]   ———. 1973. *1970 Census of Population.
Subject Reports: American Indians.* Wash-
ington, D.C.: Government Printing
Office.   (4)

*[178]   United States Commissioner of Indian
Affairs. 1954. *Annual Report of the
Commissioner of Indian Affairs.* Washing-
ton, D.C.: Government Printing Office.   (16)

[179]   United States Department of Health,
Education, and Welfare. 1974. *A Study
of Selected Socio-Economic Characteristics of
Ethnic Minorities Based on the 1970 Census.* vol. 3. *American Indians.* Washington, D.C.: Department of Health, Education, and Welfare.   (13)

[180]   Voget, Fred. 1961–62. "Introduction:
American Indians and Their Economic
Development." *Human Organization*
20:157–58.   (31)

[181]   Waddell, Jack O. 1969. *Papago Indians at Work.* Anthropological Papers, no. 2. Tucson: University of Arizona.   (23)

[182]   ———. 1975. "For Individual Power and Social Credit: The Use of Alcohol among Tucson Papagos." *Human Organization* 34:9–15.   (42)

*[183]   Waddell, Jack O., and O. Michael Watson, eds. 1971. *The American Indian in Urban Society.* Boston: Little, Brown.   (15)

[184]   Wagner, Carruth J., and Erwin S. Rabeau. 1964. "Indian Poverty and Indian Health." *United States Department of Health, Education, and Welfare Indicators,* March, pp. xxiv–xliv.   (25)

[185]   Wagner, Jean K. 1976. "The Role of Intermarriage in the Acculturation of Selected Urban American Indian Women." *Anthropologica* 18:215–29.   (22, 33)

*[186]   Wahrhaftig, Albert L. 1968. "The Tribal Cherokee Population of Eastern Oklahoma." *Current Anthropology* 9:510–18.   (13)

*[187]   Wahrhaftig, Albert L., and Robert K.
         Thomas. 1969. "Renaissance and Re-
         pression: The Oklahoma Cherokee."
         Transaction 6:42–48.   (24)

*[188]   Wax, Murray L. 1971. *Indian Americans:
         Unity and Diversity.* Englewood Cliffs,
         N.J.: Prentice-Hall.   (15)

*[189]   Weltfish, Gene. 1944. "When the In-
         dian Comes to the City." *American In-
         dian* 1:6–10.   (20)

[190]   Weppner, Robert. 1971. "Urban Eco-
         nomic Opportunities: The Example of
         Denver." In *The American Indian in
         Urban Society,* ed. Jack O. Waddell and
         O. Michael Watson, pp. 245–73. Bos-
         ton: Little, Brown.   (21)

[191]   ———. 1972. "Socioeconomic Barriers
         to Assimilation of Navajo Migrants."
         Human Organization 31:303–14.   (28, 30, 50)

[192]   Wilkie, Jane Riblett. 1976. "The United
         States Population by Race and Urban-
         Rural Residence 1790–1970: Reference
         Tables." *Demography* 13:139–48.   (26)

[193]   Wilms, Douglas C. 1974. "Cherokee
         Settlement Patterns in Nineteenth Cen-

tury Georgia." *Southeastern Geographer* 14:46–53.   (10)

[194] Wilson, C. Roderick. 1969. "Papago Indian Population Movement: An Index of Cultural Change." *Rocky Mountain Social Science Journal* 6:23–32.   (26)

[195] Withycombe, Jeraldine S. 1973. "Relationships of Self-Concept, Social Status, and Self-Perceived Social Status and Racial Differences of Paiute Indian and White Elementary School Children." *Journal of Social Psychology* 91:337–38.   (47)

[196] Wood, W. Raymond. 1974. "Northern Plains Village Cultures: Internal Stability and External Relationships." *Journal of Anthropological Research* 30:1–16.   (9)

[197] Yinger, J. Milton, and George Eaton Simpson. 1978. "The Integration of Americans of Indian Descent." *Annals of the American Academy of Political and Social Science* 436:137–51.   (49, 50)

[198] Young, James R., Dennis Moristo, and David Tenebaum. 1976. *An Inventory of the Mission Indian Agency Records.* American Indian Treaties Publication Series, no. 3. Los Angeles: American Indian Studies Center, University of California.   (3)

The Newberry Library
Center for the History of the American Indian
Founding Director: D'Arcy McNickle
Director: Francis Jennings

Established in 1972 by the Newberry Library, in conjunction with the Committee on Institutional Cooperation of eleven midwestern universities, the Center makes the resources of one of America's foremost research libraries in the Humanities available to those interested in improving the quality and effectiveness of teaching American Indian history. The Newberry's collections include some 110,000 volumes on the history of the American Indian and offer specialized resources for studying historical aspects of Indian-White relations and Indian linguistics. The Center also assists Native Americans engaged in writing tribal histories and developing educational materials.

ADVISORY COMMITTEE

Chairman: Alfonso Ortiz
University of New Mexico